Unleash your inner badness!

Be a Bad Girl

A Journal

by Cameron Tuttle

Illustrations by Susannah Bettag

CHRONICLE BOOKS

ISBN 0-8118-3191-4

Printed in Hong Kong

Illustrations by Susannah Bettag
Design by Pamela Geismar

10 9 8 7 6 5 4 3 2

Distributed in Canada by
Raincoast Books
9050 Shaughnessy Street
Vancouver, B.C. V6P 6E5

Chronicle Books LLC
85 Second Street
San Francisco, CA 94105
www.chroniclebooks.com

Visit www.badgirlswirl.com
to mix it up with other bad girls!

If you're holding this journal in your hottie little hands, you're already on the road to self-funfillment. And that's what becoming a bad girl is all about!

This *Be a Bad Girl* journal will keep you company and inspire you like your favorite bad girl friend. As you learn to explore, exploit, and embrace you at your uncensored best, you'll unleash your inner badness with style.

But that's not all! This journal is also a sly little secret weapon. If you want to impress someone, just leave this sitting out in plain view. Snoopers will find it, read it (they always do), and be wowed by your bold, beautiful badness.

How many more reasons do you need? Get started! And soon you will be caught up in the Bad Girl Swirl . . . .

Explore Your Bad Girl

How to Find Your

Being a bad girl isn't about breaking the law. It's about breaking the rules—and respecting yourself in the morning. It's about pushing back, pushing the envelope, and pushing yourself to new limits. It's about not being afraid to use your head, your heart, or your honey pot to get what you want.

A bad girl is you at your uncensored best—whoever you are, whatever your style. Finding your badness requires nothing more than an easy attitude adjustment. To dial it up, just lock and load these power phrases in your mind:

"I rule!"

"I rock!"

"I know what I want and how to get it!" (Or at least how to have fun trying!)

Remember: Being a bad girl isn't about getting more stuff, it's about getting more satisfaction.

Badness

Admit it. You want more satisfaction. Now get specific. What makes you feel alive? What makes you thrive? What gets your motor running? Write your immediate responses here (don't think, sweetcakes, just emote onto the page):

_____

_____

_____

_____

_____

_____

_____

_____

_____

_____

_____

_____

_____

_____

_____

_____

_____

_____

Bad Girl Goal: Talk the talk, walk the walk, live the dream. Know that you can get all of this—and more!

Getting into the Swirl

When you get really good at being bad, you'll be living in the Bad Girl Swirl—the getting-it zone, that magical place in time where everything comes together and goes your way. When you're in the swirl, you're in your element and in your groove. You're feeling good, you've got the power, you've got your mojo, you're hitting your stride and hitting the sweet spot.

To find your way into the Bad Girl Swirl, do a quick self-exploration:

My mojo makers:

_____

_____

_____

_____

_____

_____

_____

_____

My power boosters:

_____

_____

_____

_____

_____

_____

_____

_____

_____

_____

My spot sweeteners:

_____

_____

_____

_____

_____

_____

_____

_____

_____

_____

_____

_____

_____

When I see myself in the swirl, I'm doing . . .

. . . person:

. . . place:

_____

_____

_____

_____

_____

_____

_____

_____

_____

_____

. . . thing:

_____

_____

_____

_____

_____

_____

_____

_____

_____

_____

_____

_____

Snap out of it! There's a bad girl inside every girl. You may not feel it. You may not believe it. But she's there. Dig up some old photo albums from your childhood. Look at pictures of yourself when you were ten or twelve, seven or eight, four or five. Go back as far as you have to go to find the impish grin, the sparkly eyes, the girl in ridiculous outfits that only she could love and appreciate. Look for the smirk, look for the fire, look for the little girl who didn't know enough to be afraid of her own wants. When you spot that little bad girl, you'll know it. Zero in on her loving-life vibe and you'll be good to go.

For inspiration, insert your favorite little bad girl photo from your childhood here ——————————————→

Bad Girl Goal: Forget the sweet inner child, unleash your inner wild and make that little bad girl proud!

Badness Potential?

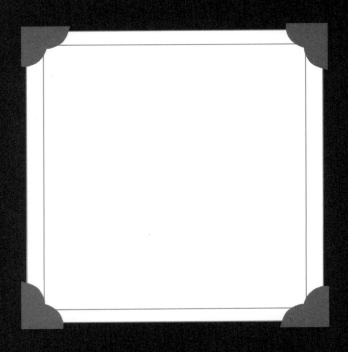

My Bad Girl Past

When I was a kid, what I wanted most/got in trouble for wanting/broke the rules to get was . . .

_____

_____

_____

_____

_____

_____

_____

_____

_____

Ditto for junior high . . .

_____

_____

_____

_____

_____

_____

_____

_____

_____

Ditto for high school . . .

_____

_____

_____

_____

_____

_____

_____

_____

_____

_____

Ditto for college . . .

_____

_____

_____

_____

_____

_____

_____

_____

_____

_____

_____

The school-age bad girl **pranks** and **brushes with the law**
that made me famous among my friends . . .

The single best **bad girl story** from my youth is . . .

Craziest **stunts I got away with** (and still made it home by curfew) in order of badness:

5. *only semi-bad* _____

_____

_____

_____

4. _____

_____

_____

_____

3. *pretty bad* _____

_____

_____

_____

2. _____

_____

_____

_____

1. *most very bad* _____

_____

_____

_____

_____

_____

Bad girls in my class I admired or **wanted to be**:

1. _____

2. _____

3. _____

4. _____

5. _____

6. _____

7. _____

8. _____

9. _____

10. _____

My **best bad girl friends** of my childhood:

1. _____

| Where she | Where she probably |
| is now: | expected me to end up: |

_____ _____

_____ _____

_____ _____

_____ _____

2. _____

| Where she | Where she probably |
| is now: | expected me to end up: |

_____ _____

_____ _____

_____ _____

_____ _____

3. _____

| Where she | Where she probably |
| is now: | expected me to end up: |

_____ _____

_____ _____

_____ _____

_____ _____

4. _____

Where she
is now:

Where she probably
expected me to end up:

_____   _____

_____   _____

_____   _____

_____   _____

5. _____

Where she
is now:

Where she probably
expected me to end up:

_____   _____

_____   _____

_____   _____

_____   _____

6. _____

Where she
is now:

Where she probably
expected me to end up:

_____   _____

_____   _____

_____   _____

_____   _____

Be Bad Now

Now that you're grown up (sort of), you can be every bit as naughty as you were or wanted to be as a kid. In fact, you can be even naughtier. Now you've got the freedom to set your own curfew, make your own choices, and hold your own remote.

Insert a current bad girl photo here for inspiration. Don't have one? Go get one! ⟶

Bad Girl Goal: Make my Bad Girl Future exceed everyone's expectations—starting now!

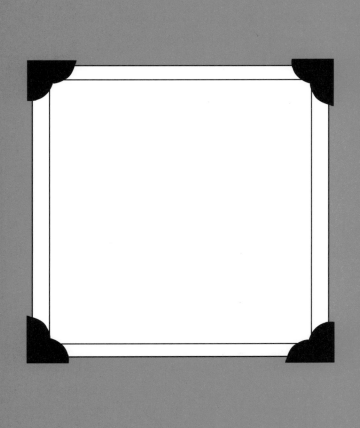

My Bad Girl Present

Now that I'm a grown-up, what I want most/get in trouble for wanting/would bend the law to get is . . .

_____

_____

_____

_____

_____

_____

_____

_____

The most recent bad girl **pranks** and **brushes with the law** that have made me famous among my friends and coworkers . . .

_____

_____

_____

_____

_____

_____

_____

_____

_____

The single best **bad girl story** from this month is . . .

_____

_____

_____

_____

_____

_____

_____

_____

_____

_____

_____

_____

_____

_____

_____

_____

_____

_____

_____

_____

_____

_____

Craziest stunts I got away with (and still made it to work the next day) in order of badness:

5. *only semi-bad* _____

_____

_____

_____

4. _____

_____

_____

3. *pretty bad* _____

_____

_____

2. _____ .

_____

_____

1. *most very bad* _____

_____

_____

_____

The bad girls in my **personal posse** I admire or want to be:

1. _____

2. _____

3. _____

4. _____

5. _____

6. _____

7. _____

8. _____

9. _____

10. _____

My **best bad girl friends** right now:

1. _____

Where she'll be
in ten years:

Where she probably
expects me to end up:

_____   _____

_____   _____

_____   _____

_____   _____

2. _____

Where she'll be
in ten years:

Where she probably
expects me to end up:

_____   _____

_____   _____

_____   _____

_____   _____

3. _____

Where she'll be
in ten years:

Where she probably
expects me to end up:

_____   _____

_____   _____

_____   _____

_____   _____

4. _____

Where she'll be
in ten years:

Where she probably
expects me to end up:

_____   _____

_____   _____

_____   _____

_____   _____

5. _____

Where she'll be
in ten years:

Where she probably
expects me to end up:

_____   _____

_____   _____

_____   _____

_____   _____

6. _____

Where she'll be
in ten years:

Where she probably
expects me to end up:

_____   _____

_____   _____

_____   _____

_____   _____

The Informational

Struggling to think of any recent bad girl behavior? No idea what you really want from life? You could be suffering from Bad Girl Block. Fortunately, there's a quick and painless cure. Just whip up a Bad Girl Cocktail and conduct an informational interview with yourself. Take a swallow or two, then answer the following questions with no censoring, no analyzing, no compromising. You'll awaken the inner wild and get your bad girl juices flowing!

How to Make a Bad Girl Cocktail

1 ½ oz. Absolut Mandrin
¼ oz. Peach Schnapps (Chicks love it!)
1 oz. Sweet and Sour
½ oz. Cranberry juice

Mix in a shaker with ice. Serve straight up in a martini glass with a lightly sugared rim and a slice of lemon. Drink with attitude.

Interview

1. What would you do if no one was ever looking?

(Pssssst: No one else really cares what you do; they're too busy worrying about what they should do.)

2. What would you do if money didn't matter?

(Pssssst: When you're living in the Bad Girl Swirl, it doesn't.)

_____

_____

_____

_____

_____

_____

_____

_____

_____

3. What would you do if you didn't have to explain it on a resumé?

(Pssssst: You don't. Besides, you'll be much more interesting if your resumé reads like an adventure novel.)

_____

_____

_____

_____

_____

_____

_____

_____

4. What would you do if no one could stop you?

(Pssssst: No one can, unless you let them.)

5. What would you do if you knew you were going to die?

(Duh!)

_____

_____

_____

_____

_____

_____

_____

_____

6. What would you do if you weren't such a chicken?

(Let's find out.)

_____

_____

_____

_____

_____

_____

_____

_____

_____

If you've made it to the bottom of the list and the bottom of your glass, your bad girl self should be coming to life. Now mix yourself another cocktail and ask her the same questions and see if your answers are getting badder.

Bad Girl Goal: Be so honest your answers will make snoopers blush.

Lose Your Good Girl

Are you a virtual virgin in key bad girl areas? Then it's time to pop the cherry and earn some bad girl stripes. Start by reviewing the list of activities below. If you've done it, check it. If you haven't done it, don't be sad, get bad! If you've inspired someone else to do it, check it twice.

Then, describe what transpired while losing your virtual virginity on each. (Did you rope someone into doing it with you? Did you meet a cute stranger while doing it? Did it give you a rush? Will it stay on your record?)

I have . . .

❑ used an alias _____

_____

_____

_____

_____

❑ acted on a wild impulse _____

_____

_____

_____

_____

_____

Virginity

☐ ignored the rules _____

_____
_____
_____
_____
_____

☐ jaywalked _____

_____
_____
_____
_____

☐ indulged my desires _____

_____
_____
_____
_____

☐ challenged an authority figure _____

_____
_____
_____
_____

❏ bought expensive, impractical shoes ─────────────

_____

_____

_____

_____

❏ used unconventional wisdom ────────────────

_____

_____

_____

_____

_____

❏ said "no!" ───────────────────────────────

_____

_____

_____

_____

_____

❏ called in sick and gone to the beach ────────────

_____

_____

_____

_____

❑ shopped shamelessly _____

_____

_____

_____

❑ mastered creative parking _____

_____

_____

❑ practiced random acts of exhibitionism _____

_____

_____

_____

_____

❑ borrowed my roommate's clothes _____

_____

_____

_____

❑ stolen kisses _____

_____

_____

_____

_____

❑ had casual sex ————————————————

———————————————————————————

———————————————————————————

———————————————————————————

———————————————————————————

❑ had black-tie sex ———————————————

———————————————————————————

———————————————————————————

———————————————————————————

———————————————————————————

❑ been a social stalker ————————————

———————————————————————————

———————————————————————————

———————————————————————————

———————————————————————————

———————————————————————————

❑ accumulated vices, virtual or otherwise ——

———————————————————————————

———————————————————————————

———————————————————————————

———————————————————————————

❑ made crank calls —————————————

———————————————————————————

———————————————————————————

———————————————————————————

———————————————————————————

❏ gotten booty-call waiting ——————————————

_____
_____
_____
_____

❏ eavesdropped and retold fab tales as my own ————

_____
_____
_____
_____

❏ worn stop-traffic sexy clothes ——————————

_____
_____
_____
_____

❏ made out at work ——————————————————

_____
_____
_____
_____
_____
_____

❏ worn invisible underwear —————————————————

——
——
——
——

❏ been a bad influence on friends ——————————

——
——
——
——
——

❏ danced naked in front of a mirror ——————————

——
——
——
——

❏ backed into a meter maid ——————————————

——
——
——
——
——

Surely you've discovered tons of new ways to push your badness boundaries besides these. Name your new favorite bad
girl activities here:

❑ _____
_____
_____
_____
_____

❑ _____
_____
_____
_____
_____

❑ _____
_____
_____
_____

❑ _____
_____
_____
_____
_____

*Bad Girl Goal: Attempt three new activities this week.
Repeat frequently until mastered.*

Typical Bad Girl's

As you work your way into the Bad Girl Swirl, you'll find that your whole outlook on life changes—from what to buy at the grocery store to what you use as your personal mantra. Want to see your progress? Follow this example, chart it here, and return each week to see the improvements!

Awakened by:

WEEK 1	*recurring anxiety dream*
WEEK 2	*recurring sex dream*
WEEK 3	*recurring sex*

Transformation

	First thought of the day:
WEEK 1	*I'm already late.*
WEEK 2	*I'm already happy.*
WEEK 3	*I'm so happy I don't care if I'm late.*
	(Besides, schedules are for suckers.)

To-do list:

WEEK 1

Gym
Ignore desires
Buy fruits & vegetables

_____
_____
_____
_____

WEEK 2

Sleep late
Explore desires
Buy banana & cucumber

_____
_____
_____
_____

WEEK 3

Sleep late with Jim
Indulge desires
Buy vibrator

_____
_____
_____
_____
_____

Self-image:

WEEK 1

If I were thinner, I'd be better.

_____
_____
_____
_____
_____
_____
_____

WEEK 2

If I were thinner, I'd be bitter.

_____
_____
_____
_____
_____
_____
_____

WEEK 3

I'm so foxy, I'm attracted to myself!

_____
_____
_____
_____
_____
_____
_____

Attitude:

WEEK 1

If I don't get what I want, I don't deserve it.

_____

_____

_____

_____

_____

_____

WEEK 2

If I don't get what I want, I haven't tried hard enough.

_____

_____

_____

_____

_____

WEEK 3

If I don't get what I want, I deserve something much better.

_____

_____

_____

_____

_____

_____

Big worry:

WEEK 1	*Am I scraping my tongue properly?*
	_____
	_____
	_____
	_____
	_____
	_____
WEEK 2	*Will anyone notice if I forget to return to work after my three-martini lunch?*
	_____
	_____
	_____
	_____
	_____
WEEK 3	*Am I going to catch something stealing sips from other people's drinks?*
	_____
	_____
	_____
	_____
	_____
	_____

Secret life plan:

WEEK 1
If I find a husband I love, I'll never need to work again.

_____
_____
_____
_____
_____

WEEK 2
If I find a job I love, I'll never need to find a husband.

_____
_____
_____
_____
_____

WEEK 3
If I find my badness, I'll never need anything—except accomplices.

_____
_____
_____
_____
_____

Mantra:

WEEK 1 *I will survive, I will survive.*

_____
_____
_____
_____
_____
_____

WEEK 2 *I will thrive, I will thrive.*

_____
_____
_____
_____
_____
_____

WEEK 3 *I am queen bee of the hive.*

_____
_____
_____
_____
_____
_____

Religious outlook:

WEEK 1

Lord help me.

_____

_____

_____

_____

_____

_____

_____

WEEK 2

God bless America.

_____

_____

_____

_____

_____

_____

_____

WEEK 3

God is a Bad Girl!

_____

_____

_____

_____

_____

_____

_____

Sex life:

WEEK 1

I'm too stressed to even think about it.

WEEK 2

Is it hot in here? Or could it be global warming?

WEEK 3

I'm so hot, I could be causing global warming!

Life's big question:

WEEK 1

Why am I alive?

_____

_____

_____

_____

_____

_____

WEEK 2

*Why have I lived so long without satin
    sheets?*

_____

_____

_____

_____

_____

WEEK 3

*Why do people leave bed at all when it's
    such a nice place to entertain?*

_____

_____

_____

_____

_____

Today's highlights:

WEEK 1

Ate fat-free all day.
Saved $1.12 buying TP in bulk.
Made amends at work.

_____

_____

_____

_____

WEEK 2

Ate for free all day.
Saved $6.12 lifting TP from the office.
Made a mess at work.

_____

_____

_____

_____

WEEK 3

Ate for three all day.
TP'd my ex's car and boss's house.
Made out at work.

_____

_____

_____

_____

Notes on Your Exploration

Now it's time to reflect on what you've learned in this section. Use these pages for stream-of-unconsciousness scribbles, freebie-associating, or deep tissue mental massages.

Exploit Your Bad Girl

Getting a Life

Being a bad girl is not just a trendy lifestyle, it's a trendy way of living. But living the life you want and having fun doing it never goes out of style.

Why You Really Want a Bad Girl's Life

* Little things don't bug you as much

* You'll rule at your high school reunion

* Justifies big bar tabs at swanky spots

* You get to wonder who will play you in the movie

* You talk to your parents less

* You can be lots of new people without having to date them

* Juicy journal entries make for great posthumous publishing

* Perfect distraction from Why-Are-We-Here woes

* Feel less guilty about your cell-phone bill

* It won't take a month for someone to find you if you die in your sleep

Building Your Bad Girl

Now that you have a sense of your bad girl self and what she wants, it's time to get organized, make a plan, and make yourself bad as you want to be!

Building the foundation of your bad girl self is like building a successful brand. It takes vision, strategy, planning, and hard work. The following is a simple exercise to help you become the bad girl of your dreams. Be honest, be shameless, be proud to be bad!

The Bad Girl

Vision *(How do I see my bad girl self in the future?)*

_____

_____

_____

_____

_____

_____

_____

_____

_____

Mission *(What's my unique purpose in the bad girl universe?)*

_____

_____

_____

_____

_____

_____

_____

_____

_____

_____

_____

Planner

Key Objectives *(What must I accomplish to achieve my bad girl goals?)*

_____

_____

_____

_____

_____

_____

_____

_____

Strategies *(How can I get what my bad girl self wants over time?)*

_____

_____

_____

_____

_____

_____

_____

_____

_____

_____

Goals *(What specific things must I do to be a success-ful bad girl?)*

_____

_____

_____

_____

_____

_____

_____

_____

_____

Personal Tagline *(What's a catchy, consumer-friendly phrase that summarizes my bad girl mission?)*

_____

_____

_____

_____

_____

_____

_____

_____

_____

_____

Personal Tagline Ideas

You can change your personal tagline as often as you change your mind or your shoes. Some taglines can last a lifetime (and should); others have a one-date shelf life. When selecting your personal tagline, be creative, be courageous, and be true to your heart's desire.

* Dangerous at any speed

* Wanted in every western state

* So funny it hurts

* Everywhere you want me to be

* Hot-landish!

* Super fly in every guy's eye

* Drink different

* Bad to the bone

* Come to Mama

* I am not a drinking game

* Over 4 million kisses served

* Exercising my stalk options

* Just do him

Bad Girl Alias

Another thing every bad girl needs is an alias. It's your quick-release tool to get out of your everyday rut and into your bad girl groove in seconds. Choose an alias that makes you feel silly, sassy, flashy, sexy, exotic, or whatever gives you the freedom to bust loose, the confidence to break your own rules, and the cover you need when making a quick getaway. How do you begin to choose? Try the exercise below:

Write down the names of:

The girls you envied in high school:

_____   _____

_____   _____

Your favorite soap opera characters:

_____   _____

_____   _____

Your favorite literary vixens:

_____   _____

_____   _____

Your favorite bad girls from history:

_____   _____

_____   _____

Also write down the names of:

Your favorite glam-rock bands:

_____   _____

_____   _____

Your favorite couture designers:

_____   _____

_____   _____

Your favorite carnival rides:

_____   _____

_____   _____

Then mix it up, picking one from each page, until you find an alias that fits like your favorite leopard-print panties. You could be Ashley Tilt-a-Whirl, Parker Poison, Eve Zipper, Donatella Bovary!

Your Bad Girl Aliases:

1._____

2._____

3._____

4._____

5._____

6._____

7._____

Instant Alias Finder

If you're facing Bad Girl Block, try these instant alias finders:

	First Name	**Last Name**
Your Porn Star Name	the name of your first pet	your mother's maiden name
Your Soap Opera Name	your middle name	the name of the first street where you lived
Your Road Trip Name	what you had for breakfast	where you last peed beside the road
Your Dating Diva Name	something sweet within sight	any liquid in your kitchen
Your Girl Detective Name	favorite baby animal	where you last went to school
Your Barfly Name	the last snack food you ate	your favorite drink

You can call me . . .

_____

_____

_____

_____

_____

_____

_____

_____

_____

_____

_____

_____

_____

_____

_____

_____

_____

Bad Girl Goal: Choose an alias and make it your own.
Use it after hours all week long.

Dating Bad Girl

Of course, you don't need a man, but sometimes you want one. Maybe you're moving heavy furniture, trying to change your oil, or installing a DSL line. Whatever your motivation, it's probably not the typical good girl reason. You're not looking for the tall handsome husband, the 2.5 kids, and the constant Prozac-free positive lifestyle. You just want some fun—pronto!

Why a Bad Girl Wants to Date:

* Free food

* You get to pretend you're someone else

* Easy to be the best-dressed

* Someone can fill you in on what you missed when you left the movie to pee

* You'll go crazy if you never leave the house

* Easy way to make mom disapprove

* You can meet lots of new people without having to see them in meetings at work

* Free sex

* You get hilarious stories to tell your friends and coworkers

Style

A bad girl on the prowl must learn the difference between a bad date, a good date, and a bad girl date. Bad girl dates come in all shapes and sizes—and they're always the most fun. Your bad girl date could be a fabulous evening of scamming freebies, stealing kisses, getting your way—or ditching your date entirely and hooking up later with your girls. It's all up to you. Describe in juicy detail and rank your most recent . . .

Date_____   **Bad Date**   **Good Date**   **Bad Girl Date**

                            ❏   ❏   ❏

Description: _____

_____

_____

_____

_____

_____

_____

_____

_____

_____

_____

_____

_____

Date _____ **Bad Date**   **Good Date**   **Bad Girl Date**

❑   ❑   ❑

Description: _____

_____

_____

_____

_____

_____

_____

_____

_____

Date _____ **Bad Date**   **Good Date**   **Bad Girl Date**

❑   ❑   ❑

Description: _____

_____

_____

_____

_____

_____

_____

_____

_____

_____

Date ———————— **Bad Date**   **Good Date**   **Bad Girl Date**

                      ❑   ❑   ❑

Description: _____

_____

_____

_____

_____

_____

_____

_____

_____

Date ———————— **Bad Date**   **Good Date**   **Bad Girl Date**

                      ❑   ❑   ❑

Description: _____

_____

_____

_____

_____

_____

_____

_____

_____

Bad Girl Goal: Turn next date, no matter how dull, into a bad girl date. Avoid incarceration.

Dating Yourself

Dating yourself can sometimes be the most satisfying way to date. You know from the start that you're building a relationship that will last. You don't have to worry about infidelity. You always get to choose the restaurant and you win every argument. Plus, you can still put out as much as you please and never be labeled a nympho slut!

What's your ideal date? Describe it here:

_____

_____

_____

_____

_____

_____

_____

_____

_____

_____

_____

_____

_____

_____

Take yourself out on that date this week, and write down all the ways it was better than any actual dates in recent memory:

_____

_____

_____

_____

_____

_____

_____

_____

_____

_____

_____

_____

_____

_____

_____

_____

_____

_____

_____

Bad Girl Goal: Take yourself on a satisfying dream date with all the trimmings one night per month.

Be a Bad Girl Mentor

As you work towards becoming badder, you can score extra points by helping someone else to be bad. If you know someone at risk of being a good girl for the rest of her life, reach out to her and become a bad girl mentor.

Girls who've helped me be a badder girl:

* _____
* _____
* _____
* _____
* _____
* _____
* _____
* _____
* _____
* _____

Girls in desperate need of my help to be badder . . .

*
*
*
*
*
*
*
*
*
*

. . . and the ways I plan to recruit them:

*
*
*
*
*
*
*
*
*
*

Bad Girl Goal: Convert three good girls this week and
reward them when they show real signs of progress.

Name: _____
Progress: _____
_____
_____
_____

Reward: _____
_____

Name: _____
Progress: _____
_____
_____
_____

Reward: _____
_____

Name: _____
Progress: _____
_____
_____
_____

Reward: _____
_____

Helpful Hints for Bad Girls in Training

Reward yourself or other young Bad Girls in Training (BGITs) with a bad girl merit badge for every new skill or bad girl quality mastered. Check off the suggested BGIT badges as you achieve them:

❑ laughed at myself

❑ ran through the sprinklers in party clothes

❑ used a loud fart whoopee cushion in a library, church, or temple

❑ bought expensive impractical shoes

❑ followed my heart

❑ fooled someone with trick ring and squirted water up their nose

❑ danced around and found the boogie in my butt

❑ trusted my instincts

❑ talked about something taboo

❑ made a disguise with a pantyliner

❑ climbed a tree in a dress wearing invisible underwear

❑ followed my dreams

❑ blew up a Barbie

Notes on Your Exploitation

Now it's time to reflect on what you've learned in this section.
Use these pages for stream-of-unconsciousness scribbles,
freebie-associating, or deep tissue mental massages.

_____

_____

_____

_____

_____

_____

_____

_____

_____

_____

_____

_____

_____

_____

_____

_____

_____

_____

_____

_____

_____

_____

Embrace Your Bad Girl

Bad Girl Friends

The key to embracing a great bad girl life is great bad girl friends. Choose them wisely. A real bad girl friend is not only there for you—she's good for you. Honor the bad girl friends in your personal posse by recording their public accomplishments and their naughty little secrets. Be sure to include key details: name, best alias, claim to badness fame, best bad girl scams, incriminating photo.

Bad Girl Friend

Name: _____

Best alias: _____

Claim to badness fame: _____

_____

_____

_____

Best bad girl scam: _____

_____

_____

_____

Incriminating photo:

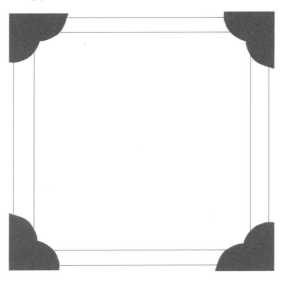

Bad Girl Friend

Name: _____

Best alias: _____

Claim to badness fame: _____

_____

_____

_____

Best bad girl scam: _____

_____

_____

_____

Incriminating photo:

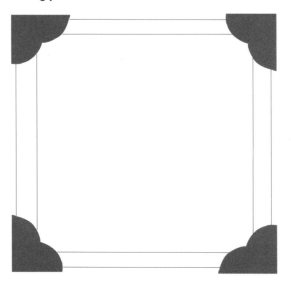

Bad Girl Friend

Name: _____

Best alias: _____

Claim to badness fame: _____

_____

_____

_____

Best bad girl scam: _____

_____

_____

_____

Incriminating photo:

Bad Girl Friend

Name: ───────────────────────────────

Best alias: ──────────────────────────

Claim to badness fame: ──────────────────

───────────────────────────────────

───────────────────────────────────

───────────────────────────────────

Best bad girl scam: ────────────────────

───────────────────────────────────

───────────────────────────────────

───────────────────────────────────

Incriminating photo:

Bad Girl Friend

Name: _____

Best alias: _____

Claim to badness fame: _____

_____

_____

_____

Best bad girl scam: _____

_____

_____

_____

Incriminating photo:

Bad Girlfriends

We've all mistaken a bad girlfriend for a bad girl friend. When you erroneously invite an evil back-stabber or a depressing loser into your inner circle, the results can be devastating. This girl must be flushed from the swirl, pronto! Describe the horrors of your bad girlfriend experience—and the way you successfully dumped her.

_____

_____

_____

_____

_____

_____

_____

_____

_____

_____

_____

_____

_____

_____

_____

_____

Bad Girlfriends vs. Bad Girl Friends
Know the difference and how to deal.

A Bad Girlfriend

Thinks of you as a rival

Will steal your man if
you're not careful

Talks about the size of
your ass at work

Will dump you in a flash
if she gets a boyfriend

Tells you it's immature
to do a drive-by

Tells you things she
knows will hurt

Flirts with your boyfriend

Dates your ex without a
second thought

Doesn't take any respon-
sibility for her shit

A Bad Girl Friend

Thinks of you as a rebel

Will steal your drink if
you're not careful

Covers your ass at work

Will be there in a flash
if you get dumped

Rides shotgun when you
do a drive-by

Tells it like it is, even
when it hurts

Farts with your boyfriend

Hates your ex without
a second thought

Doesn't take any shit

A bad girlfriend is no friend at all. Lose her fast, and don't
lose a minute wondering if you did the right thing. A bad
girl friend is a keeper. She keeps you laughing, keeps you
strong, and keeps you in touch with your best bad girl self.

Bad Girl Out-of-

To bond with your favorite bad girls, gather them together and, after a few drinks, read the following questions aloud. Pass the journal and have each person write down her answers. (Lefties use right hand; righties use left hand.) Then read the answers to the group, one question at a time, and try to figure out who's who.

1. Favorite bad girl of all time:

_____

_____

_____

_____

_____

_____

_____

_____

_____

_____

_____

_____

_____

Focus Group

2. What do you really want in life?

3. What do you secretly want that you don't want anyone to know you want?

4. How have you used your badness to get what you want?

5. What's the bad girl episode you're most proud of?

6a. What's the baddest thing you've ever done in a bar?

6b. What's the baddest thing you've ever done in a car?

6c. What's the baddest thing you've ever done in a cubicle?

6d. What's the baddest thing you've ever done in your parents' bed?

_____

_____

_____

_____

_____

_____

_____

_____

_____

_____

_____

_____

_____

_____

_____

_____

_____

_____

_____

_____

_____

_____

6e. What's the baddest thing you've ever done on a plane?

Perception is

Being a bad girl is not just about what you do, but how you choose to see what you do. If you can learn the power of the quickie mental upgrade, you'll feel better—and badder—in seconds. Here are some examples to get you started:

Good Girl Reality

I can't afford to do laundry. ———————

I have no idea what I'm doing with my life. ———————

I'm broke. ———————

I'm flabby. ———————

I'm between jobs. ———————

I'm always single. ———————

All my clothes are really old. ———————

I can't balance my checkbook. ———————

I'm a temp. ———————

I work out of my studio apartment. ———————

I'm a pathetic loser. ———————

I live in a basement. ———————

Everything

Bad Girl Mental Upgrade

→ I'm so boho chic.

→ I'm a free spirit.

→ I have a cash flow problem.

→ I'm fluffy.

→ I'm on hiatus.

→ I'm too wildly independent to be in a relationship.

→ I'm so retro!

→ I'm a creative genius.

→ I'm a mercenary in the war against data processing.

→ I work in suite 7B.

→ I'm an artistic loner.

→ I live in a garden apartment.

See how easy it is? Now you try it! When you're in a funk, use the previous examples as a guide and write down what's bugging you and how a bad girl should really look at it:

My Good Girl Reality

_____

_____

_____

_____

_____

_____

_____

_____

_____

_____

_____

_____

_____

_____

_____

My Bad Girl Mental Upgrade

→ _____
→ _____
→ _____
→ _____
→ _____
→ _____
→ _____
→ _____
→ _____
→ _____
→ _____
→ _____
→ _____
→ _____

Storytelling 101

Even more fun than how you see yourself is how other people see you! Routine events in your life take on new excitement when you make them into outrageous, embellished stories.

Write down **one average scene** from this week (you got a parking ticket, had a dull date, led a meeting at work):

_____

_____

_____

_____

_____

_____

Now craft an **outrageous bad girl story** around it:

_____

_____

_____

_____

_____

_____

_____

_____

_____

_____

_____

_____

_____

_____

_____

_____

_____

_____

_____

Bad Girl Goal: Tell the story to three unsuspecting
people this week. (Remember: Bad is in the details.)
Record their reactions here:

_____

_____

_____

_____

_____

_____

_____

_____

_____

_____

Of course, this skill also works for dates, job interviews, and phone calls to your parents. Use this space to practice:

On a Date:

Say it's going nowhere; you want to bail and meet your bad girl friends at a bar across town. What do you tell your date?

At a Job Interview:

Say you spent the last six months as a temp, and you left the job before that in a huff. How do you describe all this in a way that will land you the cushy job you're applying for?

With Your Parents:

Say you've got bad news to break to them—again. Like you're really not getting married, you're broke, you got fired, you totaled the car. How do you position it so it actually sounds like a coup?

_____

_____

_____

_____

_____

_____

_____

_____

_____

_____

_____

_____

_____

_____

_____

_____

_____

_____

_____

Maybe you should try that one again . . .

_____

_____

_____

_____

_____

_____

_____

_____

_____

_____

_____

_____

_____

_____

_____

_____

_____

_____

_____

_____

_____

_____

Bad Girl Goal: Practice self-glorifying tale-telling 'til you're a pro. Try on telemarketers, baristas, and strangers on the bus.

The Sacred Bad Girl

Every bad girl needs a hefty dose of self-love. When you're a bad girl, you are beautiful, every day in every way. Bad hair? Love it! Stressed out? Intense! Dark circles? Dramatic! Start with a modest daily affirmation to focus on your bad girl self-esteem. Then work up to saying these with feeling into your mirror. Then poll your favorite bad girls to come up with more!

1. "Good golly, I'm a hot tamale!"

2. "I declare, I dig my hair!"

3. "It's hip and funky looking this damn chunky!"

4. "It's no paradox that I am such a fox!"

5. "Tell your Mom, I'm the bomb!"

6. "Don't mean to be crass but I love this ass!"

7. "Hot home cookin'—I'm that good lookin'!"

8. "With eyes like mine, who needs wine!"

9. "I love my pores like warm s'mores!"

10. "Strike a pose, 'cause I adore this nose!"

11. "It's super heavy duty, being such a freakin' beauty!"

12. "You're so purty, let's get flirty!"

13. "Oh yeah honey, I'm so money!"

Affirmations

Create your own affirmations and save them:

1. _____

_____

2. _____

_____

3. _____

_____

4. _____

_____

5. _____

_____

6. _____

_____

7. _____

_____

8. _____

_____

9. _____

_____

10. _____

_____

Nice Booty, Baby!

A savvy bad girl knows that when you get a compliment—no matter what the source—you keep it! The next time you get compliments at work or on the street, whether from friends and lovers or cat-calling construction workers, jot them down here in your own personal **compliment bank.** A quick review and you'll feel loaded with self love—and maybe even a splash of self-lust!—both essential to being a bad girl.

My Compliment Bank

The best compliments I've ever received on . . .

My Brain

_____
_____
_____
_____
_____
_____
_____
_____

My Butt

_____
_____
_____
_____
_____
_____
_____
_____
_____
_____

My Sense of Humor

_____
_____
_____
_____
_____
_____
_____
_____
_____
_____

My Bad-itude

_____
_____
_____
_____
_____
_____
_____
_____
_____
_____
_____
_____

My Hair

_____
_____
_____
_____
_____
_____
_____
_____
_____
_____
_____

My Style

_____
_____
_____
_____
_____
_____
_____
_____
_____
_____
_____
_____
_____

My Legs

_____

_____

_____

_____

_____

_____

_____

_____

_____

_____

_____

My Walk

_____

_____

_____

_____

_____

_____

_____

_____

_____

_____

_____

_____

My Everything Else

How You Know You've

Are you getting there? Chart your progress with this checklist.

- ❏ I've got the coolest bad girl friends.

- ❏ I'm a bad influence.

- ❏ I'm a bad girl mentor in my community.

- ❏ I throw big bad girl parties.

- ❏ I know what I want and how to get it.

- ❏ I can moan with anticipation with the best of them.

- ❏ I'm a creative genius!

- ❏ I've lied about my age, early and often.

- ❏ I've known and loved self-lust!

- ❏ I've lovingly groped a stranger.

- ❏ I've been my own proud parent.

- ❏ I've said, "Bye, you guys!" to people I don't even know.

Become A Bad Girl

❑ I got carded on purpose!

❑ I've done inspired things with my evil ex's photo.

❑ I'm everyone's dream date!

❑ My home is a shrine to my beauty.

❑ I've used bad girl logic.

❑ My load is always balanced.

❑ I never pay for drinks unless I want to.

❑ I'm loving my life!

❑ I'm so fabulous I'm attracted to myself!

❑ Children revere me and parents fear me.

❑ I know who I am and I'm proud of it!

Bad Girl Goal: Be the girl of my wildest dreams!

Badlash! It's a

If you get criticized, attacked, or gossiped about on your way to becoming a bad girl, be proud! You're just experiencing a little badlash, which means you're definitely doing something right. Record your badlash highlights here.

My favorite badlash lines:

_____

_____

_____

_____

_____

_____

_____

_____

_____

_____

_____

_____

_____

_____

_____

_____

_____

Beautiful Thing

My baddest comebacks:

_____
_____
_____
_____
_____
_____
_____
_____
_____
_____
_____
_____
_____
_____
_____
_____
_____
_____
_____
_____
_____
_____
_____

Notes on Embracing Yourself

Now it's time to reflect on what you've learned in this section.
Use these pages for stream-of-unconsciousness scribbles,
freebie-associating, or deep tissue mental massages.

_____

_____

_____

_____

_____

_____

_____

_____

_____

_____

_____

_____

_____

_____

_____

_____

_____

_____

_____

_____

_____